BRAIN INJURIES IN
FOOTBALL

BRAIN INJURIES IN
FOOTBALL

BY STEPHANIE WATSON

CONTENT CONSULTANT
ELAD I. LEVY, MD, MBA, FACS, FAHA
PROFESSOR AND CHAIR OF NEUROSURGERY
SUNY AT BUFFALO

Essential Library
An Imprint of Abdo Publishing | www.abdopublishing.com

www.abdopublishing.com

Published by Abdo Publishing, a division of ABDO, PO Box 398166, Minneapolis, Minnesota 55439. Copyright © 2015 by Abdo Consulting Group, Inc. International copyrights reserved in all countries. No part of this book may be reproduced in any form without written permission from the publisher. Essential Library™ is a trademark and logo of Abdo Publishing.

Printed in the United States of America, North Mankato, Minnesota
042014
092014

THIS BOOK CONTAINS
RECYCLED MATERIALS

Cover Photo: Alex Brandon/AP Images
Interior Photos: Alex Brandon/AP Images, 2; Gene J. Puskar/AP Images, 6; SPL/Custom Medical Stock Photo, 11; Ben Liebenberg/AP Images, 14; Andriy Muzyka/Thinkstock, 16; Amy Myers/Shutterstock Images, 23; Al Golub/AP Images, 24; Pro Football Hall of Fame/AP Images, 27; Justin Skinner/Thinkstock, 34; Mark Mulville/The Buffalo News/AP Images, 37; Cal Sport Media/AP Images, 41; Mark Duncan/AP Images, 42; Keith Srakocic/AP Images, 45; Ben Margot/AP Images, 47; Bob Leverone/AP Images, 50; Michael Dwyer/AP Images, 54; G. Newman Lowrance/AP Images, 60; David J. Phillip/AP Images, 64; Steven Senne/AP Images, 66; Brian Cahn/Zuma Press/Newscom, 69; Bob Wellinski/The LaPorte Herald-Argus/AP Images, 74; David Drapkin/AP Images, 76; Don Wright/AP Images, 81; Elaine Thompson/AP Images, 83; Nick Wass/AP Images, 86; Brian Wallace/AP Images, 92; Peter Weber/Shutterstock Images, 95

Editor: Angela Wiechmann
Series Designer: Becky Daum

Library of Congress Control Number: 2014932557

Cataloging-in-Publication Data

Watson, Stephanie.
  Brain injuries in football / Stephanie Watson.
    p. cm. -- (Essential issues)
  Includes bibliographical references and index.
  ISBN 978-1-62403-417-6
  1. Football injuries--United States--Juvenile literature. 2. Brain--Concussion--United States--Juvenile literature.   I. Title.
  617.1--dc23

                                                              2014932557

CONTENTS

CHAPTER
ONE

IRON MIKE

When kids dream of becoming National Football League (NFL) stars, they aspire to be like Mike Webster—a true American football hero. Webster was raised on a potato farm in Tomahawk, Wisconsin. He was such a standout on his high school football team, he was recruited to play college ball. Webster played for the University of Wisconsin. Only a tiny percentage of college football players ever get drafted to the NFL. Webster was part of that elite few. He joined the Pittsburgh Steelers as a center in 1974.

Webster played football the way it was intended to be played—tough and unforgiving. He was small for a football player, measuring only six feet one (1.9 m) and weighing 215 pounds (97 kg). But he used his head like a battering ram to block much bigger players. Webster's strength and fearlessness on the field earned him the nickname "Iron Mike." He went on to play 17 seasons, winning four Super Bowl championships with the Steelers.

Mike Webster was a football legend who saw a tragic end.

In 1990, Webster retired from the NFL while he was still in his 30s. He spent some quality time with his wife and four children in their Kansas City, Missouri, dream home. He was elected to the Pro Football Hall of Fame in 1997. Life after football seemed idyllic. But under the surface, something was very wrong.

Tragedy Unfolds

Once easygoing, Webster began flying into rages at his family and friends. He suddenly became paranoid, believing people were listening in on his telephone calls and following him. He spent money without thinking, buying luxuries he could not afford, including a speedboat and a pair of motorcycles. Eventually he drained the family's bank account, and they were forced to sell their dream home.

Webster did not act or look right. When he was in his 40s, he seemed like a man far older. He limped from a damaged right heel. His right shoulder was always sore, and his knees were worn away. His fingers bent in all the wrong directions. He suffered from agonizing headaches. Webster's back hurt so much he had to sleep sitting up in a chair. Sometimes he would shoot himself with a stun gun just so he could get some rest. To make it through each day, Webster relied on a combination of drugs. He took Paxil to relieve his anxiety, Prozac to hold off depression, Ritalin to help him think clearly, and Vicodin or Darvocet to relieve his numerous aches.

The drugs didn't help him regain control of his life. His speech was incoherent. He lost his memory and was often confused. By the 1990s, the former NFL star was so lost and disoriented, he once

LITTLE HELP FROM THE NFL

In the years when there was no proof football had caused brain injuries, many former NFL players struggled to afford around-the-clock medical care. The NFL did not pay benefits to these players, as there was no proof yet the sport had caused the brain injuries and resulting symptoms.

When Webster's family tried to collect hundreds of thousands of dollars in benefits for his disabilities, the NFL claimed his disability was not from playing football. The league contended he had become disabled after retiring. The NFL initially agreed to pay him only $42,000 a year.[2] They eventually settled on $115,000 a year.[3]

left his home and slept in a Greyhound bus station in downtown Pittsburgh.

On September 24, 2002, Webster developed chest pains. He was rushed to Allegheny General Hospital in Pittsburgh, where tests showed his heart was shutting down. Webster was pronounced dead at age 50. The official cause of death was heart failure, but the last years of his life suggested something had also been terribly wrong with his brain.

Discovery in a Morgue

September 28, 2002, started out as a normal day for Bennet Omalu. As a forensic pathologist, his job was to examine dead bodies for the Allegheny County medical examiner's office in Pittsburgh. He was like a detective, trying to find out exactly how a person had died when the cause of death was uncertain.

On this particular day, the body he examined belonged to former Pittsburgh Steeler Mike Webster. Something about the case struck him as odd. The official cause of death had been a heart attack. Omalu was not a football fan, but he had seen a television story that recounted Webster's recent troubles—his drug

Finding tau protein (shown as red and pink) in Webster's brain, Omalu made a major breakthrough.

addiction and strange behavior before he died. Omalu wanted to investigate a little more deeply.

Omalu cut open the hard, bony shell of Webster's skull to reveal the brain inside. On the surface, Webster's brain looked fairly normal. But when Omalu sliced off thin sections from each part of the brain and examined them under a microscope, he was amazed by what he saw. It was full of tau protein. The substance made Webster's brain look very similar to the brain of an 85-year-old person with Alzheimer's disease, a condition that causes memory loss and affects functioning. No one had ever seen anything like this in the brain of a middle-aged football player. "I knew this was a billion-dollar kind of finding when I saw it," Omalu said.[4]

More Tragedies

Webster was not the only football player to meet a tragic end in the early 2000s. On September 30, 2004, Justin Strzelczyk, another former lineman for the Steelers, led police on a high-speed chase along Interstate 90 in New York. He rammed his pickup head-on into a tanker

25 YEARS LATER

Life after retiring from the NFL is often challenging. In 2011, Sports Illustrated checked in with 39 of the original 46 players from the 1986 Cincinnati Bengals team to see how they were doing 25 years later. The youngest was 47. The oldest was 62. Some players were doing better than others, but most of them suffered from at least one physical ailment.

Overall, nearly half of the former team members said they were having trouble with memory loss. A third of them reported daily headaches. At age 57, linebacker Reggie Williams had lost his memory. Former guard Max Montoya was only 55 at the time of the interview, but he felt as if he were living in a 70-year-old's body. "I'm deteriorating," he told Sports Illustrated.

Despite the ailments, some of the players said they would not hesitate to play professional football again if given the chance. Yet others regretted their years in the NFL. Defensive end Jim Skow said his seven seasons playing professional ball were like "trading body parts for money."[5]

truck, killing himself instantly. Family and friends said he had seemed paranoid and delusional before the incident.

In 2005, Webster's former Steelers teammate Terry Long killed himself by drinking antifreeze. It was the finale to years of mood swings, depression, and irrational business decisions. On November 20, 2006, 44-year-old Andre Waters of the Philadelphia Eagles shot himself in the head.

By the early 2000s, the dark side of football was becoming more and more apparent. Professional football players were not just retiring with sore knees and bad backs. They were becoming mentally disabled—and dying at alarming rates.

But that was not all: high school players were running onto the football field healthy and leaving on stretchers. It seemed the sport was destroying the bodies and minds of many of its players. And some people began worrying the risks of football might not be worth the glory.

CHAPTER
TWO

INSIDE
BRAIN INJURIES

Football is a game of speed, strength, and hard hits. Bones can be broken and muscles torn. But as helmets collide and crash on nearly every play, brains can also be injured. Due to its design, the brain is quite vulnerable in a high-impact sport such as football. Injuries can have immediate effects as well as long-term, life-altering repercussions.

Sophisticated but Delicate Design

The human brain is a complex system made up of more than 1 billion nerve cells called neurons, which transmit messages as quickly and efficiently as a high-speed computer. These signals control every function in the body. When a quarterback flicks his wrist as he throws a football or breathes faster as he runs, neurons are behind these actions.

In a flash, neurons transmit the messages in the brain, controlling every thought and movement of a football player like Peyton Manning.

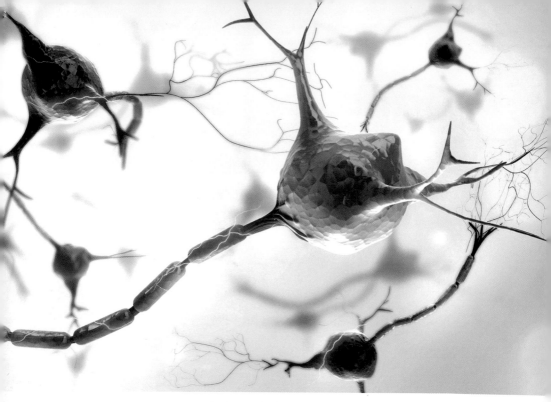

As the brain sloshes and smacks during an injury, the delicate design of a neuron can easily tear.

Zoom in on a neuron, and it looks almost like a tiny plant bulb with roots sticking out of the end. The round part is the cell body—the core of the neuron that keeps it alive. Projecting from each neuron is a long, thin shoot called an axon. Messages in the form of electric impulses travel down this shoot and pass from one neuron to another. The messages enter the next neuron through the rootlike projections, which are called dendrites. Every time a quarterback plans a new play and executes it, messages zip around from neuron to neuron.

Despite its sophisticated design, the brain is a surprisingly delicate structure. It has the consistency of Jell-O, which makes it vulnerable to damage. For protection, the brain and all its connections are immersed in a bath of fluid and surrounded by a hard, bony skull. But even these defenses are not enough to fully protect against a hard hit on the football field.

When a Football Player Takes a Hit

When a player is tackled and hits his head on the ground, what happens to the delicate brain architecture? His brain jiggles around like a mound of Jell-O, smacking against the sides of his skull. And like Jell-O, the brain does not move in a straight line. It compresses and shifts. Researchers describe this movement as slosh. The twisting and pulling movement

INSIDE THE BRAIN

The brain weighs only approximately three pounds (1.3 kg). It controls a person's every thought, movement, and behavior. The brain is divided into several parts, each with different functions. At the base of the brain is the cerebellum, which controls functions necessary to life, including breathing and heart rate.

At the top of the brain is the cerebrum, the area responsible for thinking and memory. Surrounding the cerebrum is a thin layer of brain tissue known as the cerebral cortex. This is where most of the information processing occurs in the brain. It is the human equivalent of a computer's processing unit.

can damage the neurons. They tear, breaking the connections between brain cells.

What happens to the player next depends on which part of his brain is injured. He might lose his vision, or he might have trouble remembering he is in the middle of a football game. If an area of his brain controlling balance is damaged, he could feel wobbly and dizzy when he stands up. If he was hit really hard, there is a chance he might black out and become unconscious.

Concussions

When a brain injury affects functions such as vision, memory, or balance, it is called a traumatic brain injury (TBI). A concussion is a type of TBI. Concussions are not easy to see. They do not show up on X rays. Common symptoms include dizziness; sensitivity to light and noise; blurred vision; changes in behavior; headache; and trouble concentrating, remembering, or sleeping. If the player shows any of these signs after an injury, he may have a concussion.

Concussions can be difficult to detect, however. Other medical conditions can cause many of the same symptoms, such as nausea and dizziness. Many people assume a football player has to lose consciousness to have a concussion. In reality, only 10 percent of athletes who get a concussion black out.[1] So when a player gets a concussion, sometimes it does not get identified and he does not get the treatment he needs.

Each year, between 1.6 million and 3.8 million TBIs, including concussions, occur in sports in the United States.[2] But that is not the whole story. The real number of brain injuries may be much higher. Many people who are injured—especially young people—do not ever report they have been hurt.

PUNCH-DRUNK SYNDROME

Similar to football, boxing is a sport in which head injuries are common. Especially in the early years, boxers often took hit after hit to the head during matches. After weeks, months, or years of pounding to the head, many boxers would start showing symptoms such as confusion, mood changes, and impulsiveness.

In 1928, Harrison Martland, a New Jersey medical examiner, called this condition "punch-drunk syndrome" because the symptoms were similar to the behaviors people exhibit when intoxicated. The technical term for this condition is dementia pugilistica.

Martland described boxers with this syndrome as dragging their legs, staggering, and walking with an unsteady gait. Likewise, fans described these boxers as "cuckoo," "goofy," or "slug nutty." Martland wrote that boxers who "keep at the game long enough" will show signs of brain injury.[3] Many of them suffered so much brain damage from other fighters' fists, they were put in mental institutions.

Decades later, the same symptoms sometimes still appear in boxers. They also appear in football players and other athletes with brain injuries.

Every season, a professional football player is hit in the head an estimated 1,500 times.[4] That means in a 10-year career, a player can sustain 15,000 hits to the head. And that does not include all the hits professional players also sustained earlier while playing at the youth league, high school, and college levels.

Fortunately, brain cells can heal. After a TBI, the player's body rushes to repair the damaged brain cells. Usually the damaged areas can be fixed. But brain cells will die if the injury is too severe or if the quarterback gets hit again before his brain has time to heal. And that is how head injuries can become very serious.

"If somebody tells you neurologically you could sustain some kind of brain damage that will go with you the rest of your life. If somebody had told me that a long time ago, I don't frankly think I would have [played]."[5]
—Harry Carson, former New York Giants linebacker

The Danger of a Second Hit

Often when a player was hit in the head in the early days of football, the coach would hold a couple fingers in front of the player. If the player could count the fingers, the coach would assume the player was all right. The player would return to the game. Sometimes football players would take some aspirin if they had a headache from their injuries.

Today doctors know how dangerous that approach can be. Most players heal completely from a concussion, as long as they get rest and do not play again until they receive medical clearance. But if a player returns to the game too early, the brain does not have a chance to heal itself. The player is at risk for a second concussion.

A second hard hit can make the brain swell. In what is called second-impact syndrome, the effects of a second concussion are significantly more severe than the effects of the first concussion.

Second-impact syndrome is especially dangerous for young players. Their brains are not mature enough to heal quickly from a first concussion. Also adding to the danger, many of the hits young people sustain are mild enough to go unnoticed

GETTING HIS BELL RUNG

For many years, most football coaches and players did not understand the true nature of concussions. Without the research and medical advancements available today, they relied on funny expressions to describe what happened when a player was hit in the head. They would say he "got his bell rung."[6] These expressions hid the seriousness of the head injuries players suffered. Because the injury was often not taken seriously, the typical response was to give the injured player pain medication and send him right back on the field.

yet significant enough to cause damage. An average of six young athletes die from second-impact syndrome each year.[7] "All athletes who suffer from second-impact syndrome end up either disabled or dead," said Dr. Jeffrey Mjaanes, medical director of the Chicago Sports Concussion Clinic at Rush, located at Rush University.[8]

Clearly, the brain is a complex organ. But the violent nature of football puts it at great risk—and has since the game's earliest days.

The youngest football players have the biggest risk of serious complications from concussions.

CHAPTER
THREE

FOOTBALL TAKES ITS TOLL

Ticket sales, merchandise, and television rights make the NFL a multibillion-dollar industry. Children idolize players such as Peyton Manning, Tom Brady, and Adrian Peterson. They pledge to be just like them when they grow up.

But football also has a violent and dangerous side. "It's what makes the game so popular," says former Dallas Cowboys linebacker Keith Brooking. "People love the battle! People love the violence!"[1] Even the words used to describe football plays—*sack*, *blitz*, *bomb*—imply someone is going to get hurt.

The violence may be exciting to watch, but it can take a terrible toll on players. Webster's doctor once asked him, "Have you been hit lately? And how often?" Webster said, "Oh, probably about 25,000 times or so." In response to a reporter's question about how many

At its core, football has always been a violent game.

concussions he had sustained over his career, Waters said he had lost count at 15.[2]

Aggressive play is not confined to professional football, either. The average high school lineman takes up to 1,500 hits to the head during each season.[3] At any age, inside all football players' brains, the damage may be mounting.

The Early Days

From the very start, football was a dangerous, brutal game. Players went out on the field with almost no protection except a thin helmet made from leather. To steal the ball from the opposing team, players used their heads and bodies as battering rams. Injuries were common—and often terrible. Spinal cords were severed. Skulls were bashed. Collarbones were snapped in two.

Players received virtually no protection from the earliest form of helmets—if they wore them at all.

In November 1905, Vernon Wise, a 17-year-old Illinois high school player, was knocked unconscious during a game. Two hours later, he died from a broken back. Wise's death was one of 19 that year alone in football.[5]

Football games were so popular at the time, they were drawing tens of thousands of fans. But some Americans began calling for an end to the sport. "The once athletic sport has degenerated into a contest that for brutality is little better than the gladiatorial combats in the arena in ancient Rome," one objector wrote in the *Beaumont Express.*[6]

The situation became so dire, President Theodore Roosevelt stepped in. He had a personal interest in the subject. His own son Theodore Jr. played for the Harvard University football team. In 1905, President Roosevelt called for an emergency summit at the White House. Coaches of the Harvard, Princeton, and Yale football teams came together to discuss ways to make the game safer.

As a result of their meeting, the Intercollegiate Athletic Association of the United States was founded in March 1906. The name was changed to the National Collegiate Athletic Association (NCAA) in 1910. To this day, the organization oversees college sports. With so many tragedies in football, the association took a close look at the rules of the game.

New Rules

In an attempt to make the game safer, the association members created new rules to protect football players. They increased the number of yards needed to make a first down from five to ten. They created the neutral zone, stopping players from colliding and trying to steal the ball between plays. They also eliminated a dangerous formation called the flying wedge that often led to severe injuries.

Most important, they made the forward pass legal, which revolutionized the game. Instead of relying on only running plays, which often end in violent tackles and collisions, teams could now also throw the ball down the field. These changes helped players avoid some of the contact that led to injuries.

FOOTBALL HISTORY

The sport Americans now watch and play by the millions actually evolved out of two British sports: soccer and rugby. The first US college football game was played on November 6, 1869, between Rutgers and Princeton Universities in New Jersey. But it was not yet true football. The teams played a modified version of rugby.

The man credited with launching football as Americans now know it was Walter Camp, a former Yale University rugby player. He created most of the rules high school, college, and professional football teams follow today.

When football started, it was purely amateur with local athletic clubs and college teams. Then on November 12, 1892, a Pittsburgh club paid William "Pudge" Heffelfinger $500 to play for them.[7] He became the first professional player. He also won the game on a fumble return for a touchdown.

As the number of teams grew, a league was created to organize them. In 1920, it was called the American Professional Football Conference. In 1922, the name was changed to the National Football League. In 1970, it merged with the rival American Football League to create the league as fans recognize it today.

Injuries Continue

The rule changes made the game somewhat safer, but head injuries still occurred. In the 1930s, the NCAA first acknowledged the dangers of concussions in its medical handbook. It stated concussions "should not be regarded lightly."[8] The handbook recommended players with headaches and other concussion symptoms get plenty of rest and have brain X rays to look for signs of injury. The NCAA also said players who experienced symptoms for more than 48 hours should not be allowed to compete again for "21 days or longer, if at all."[9]

Beyond college football, head injuries were also happening in professional football. By 1943, the NFL made helmets mandatory. Newer helmets in the 1950s and 1960s were made from more durable plastic, which protected players' skulls from cracking. But having a hard outer shell on their heads only made players bolder. Defensive players realized they could take down their opponents by slamming into them with the tops of their helmets. The practice became known as spearing.

Over the next few decades, rules and equipment continued to change in an effort to make football safer. Helmet manufacturers added chin straps and face masks to protect players. From the 1970s to the 2000s, the league outlawed dangerous moves such as the head slap (hitting a player on the side of his helmet) and the horse-collar tackle (grabbing an opponent's shoulder pads to tackle him). High school, college, and NFL football no longer allowed spearing.

Bigger Players, Bigger Hits

Rule and equipment changes did little to protect the giants emerging on the football field. In the 1950s, an NFL lineman might have weighed 230 pounds (104 kg). By the 2000s, an average lineman could tip the scales at nearly 350 pounds (159 kg). College players also grew, with linemen putting on approximately one to two pounds (0.4 to 0.9 kg) a year over the last 60 years.[10] More weight equals more force during a hit.

SEASON OF THE CONCUSSION

Football has always been an aggressive game. But so many NFL players had head injuries in 1994, some people called it the "Season of the Concussion."[11] The injuries occurred all season long, but October 25 was a particularly rough Sunday. Three quarterbacks—Troy Aikman of the Dallas Cowboys, Chris Miller of the Los Angeles Rams, and Vinny Testaverde of the Cleveland Browns—were knocked unconscious.

Aikman, who suffered a concussion the previous season, returned for only a few plays. The team doctor asked him the day, the month, and the year. Aikman could only answer it was Sunday.

Players were also getting faster, which increased the energy behind each hit. A scientist from the University of Nebraska calculated that a 245-pound (111 kg) linebacker could generate 1,150 pounds (522 kg) of force during a tackle.[12] Of course, a 350-pound (159 kg) player could create even more force. The potential for injury grew as the players themselves grew.

Football players were not only getting bigger. They were also encouraged to be aggressive. Their coaches preached a take-no-prisoners attitude. "I only did what I was taught to do: hit the opponent as hard as I could," said former Miami Dolphins defensive lineman Mike Golic.[13]

Players on the receiving end of these forceful hits took a pounding, often to the head. Researchers at Virginia Tech University studied how much force players absorbed during a hit. They learned an average fullback was hit approximately 27 times in each game, with a g-force of between 10 to 111 units in each hit. G-force is a measure of how much force a body receives when it is moving quickly. That many hits with that much force is "like running your head into a brick wall," said Mike Goforth, Virginia Tech's head athletic trainer.[14]

Culture of Toughness

Being able to give and take such forceful hits was considered a positive sign of toughness in football. Many players were taught to believe a concussion was the mark of a true athlete. "If I didn't have five of your so-called Grade I concussions [the mildest type of concussion] a game, that meant I was basically inactive," said San Francisco 49ers linebacker Gary Plummer.[15]

There was little concern or sympathy for injured players. Worse yet, the NFL's attitude toward head injuries trickled down to younger football players as well.

THE NUTCRACKER

Football players do not get injured only during games. Some practice drills are even more dangerous than real game play. One of the most brutal drills is called the nutcracker. The "nuts" are the players' heads cracking together. Two players smash their heads into each other at full force, and they keep smashing until one player is driven backward. The drill leaves players vulnerable to head and neck injuries.

In 2011, San Francisco 49er Eric Heitmann seriously injured his neck during a nutcracker drill. He had to miss the entire season as a result.

CHAPTER FOUR

DANGERS TO YOUNG PLAYERS

Professional football is played quickly and intensely. The players are big, and when they hit, they hit hard. It is easy to see why so many NFL players have had concussions. Yet the problem of brain injuries in football is not limited to the pros.

Roughly 3 million youth play football. More than 1 million of them play in high school, and 71,000 go on to play college ball.[1] Even the youngest players are at risk for serious brain injuries.

Tragic Headlines

A small number of injuries on high school football fields make headlines. On October 1, 2010, Nathan Stiles suffered a head injury while playing for Spring Hill High School in Kansas. His mother took him to the hospital, where he was diagnosed with a concussion. Nathan's family doctor told him not to play for a week or two.

Far too many high school football players suffer serious consequences from concussions.

Nathan did as he was told, but he was eager to return to play in the last few games of the season. Nathan's doctor cleared him to play again.

But during the final game of the season, Nathan got hit while intercepting a pass. A few minutes before half time, he staggered to the sidelines, shouting that his head hurt. As his coach went to get a trainer, Nathan collapsed. He was airlifted to a local medical center, where he died from bleeding in the brain. Nathan was just 17 years old.

Nathan was just one of many recent high school football tragedies. On October 31, 2013, Missouri high school student Chad Stover was rushed to the hospital after getting hurt in a play-off game. Two weeks later, he died. He also was 17 years old. During the same week, Charles Youvella, a high school running back from Arizona, collapsed on the field after being tackled. He died a few days later. Sixteen-year-old Damon Janes of Brocton, New York, died three days after getting hit in the head during a game.

Beyond the Headlines

But there is more to the story of brain injuries in high school football than what these headlines can tell. Each

A New York high school team observes a moment of silence for Damon Janes, who died from a head injury playing for a nearby school.

year, 43,000 to 67,000 high school football players report concussions.[2] Those numbers are higher than in any other high school team sport. And the real numbers of concussions are probably even higher. Studies show as many as half of young players who get head injuries never report them to their coaches or doctors.

More high school football players are getting brain injuries today than ever before. Teenagers were 200 percent more likely to get a concussion in 2007 than they were in 1997.[3] Some experts suggest this is due to concussions now being reported more often. But others argue it may be because players are getting bigger and faster and joining football at an earlier age.

A high school football player is roughly twice as likely to suffer a concussion than a college player. "The immature brain is still developing," explains Julian Bailes, leading neurologist and Pittsburgh Steelers team doctor. "That makes it more susceptible to damage and more likely to suffer repetitive injury."[4] Also, the injury risk is higher because many high schools do not have the protective equipment college teams use. Nor do they usually have medical experts on the sidelines to check injured players.

The Effects on Young Brains

Most high school players recover completely from a concussion, as long as they rest and do not play again until their brains heal. But those who return to the field too soon are at risk for a second concussion. The effects of second-impact syndrome are severe for young people.

In addition to sustaining major head injuries such as concussions, high school players also sustain many subconcussive hits, which are smaller. Researchers at Purdue University applied devices to helmets in order to measure players' acceleration at a high school in Lafayette, Indiana. They found players suffered subconcussive hits on almost every single play.

RECOVERING FROM A CONCUSSION

Experts on head injuries say children and teenagers who get concussions need plenty of time for their brains to heal. That may include time away not only from sports but also from school.

For the brain to heal, it needs to be as calm as possible. Any activity that stimulates the brain could slow recovery. That means young people should stay away from bright lights, television, video games, and even homework. The American Pediatric Association (APA) recommends a leave of absence from school or at least a simplified, reduced school day.

Experts say youth should not return to school and sports until doctors have verified their brains have fully healed. Even then, youth should be eased back into sports, with doctors and coaches closely watching for returning symptoms as activity progresses. The APA promotes the slogan, "When in doubt, sit them out!"[6]

Young people with long-term or frequent concussion problems may need to play less risky sports or drop out of sports entirely to avoid the serious risks of more brain injuries.

Subconcussive hits do not cause symptoms as concussions do, but they can still leave permanent damage in the brain. The effects of these injuries are largely unknown. High school football players who sustain these smaller hits usually go right back into the game afterward. That could lead to even more injury.

The Danger Continues in College

In college, players are bigger, stronger, and faster than they were in high school. That means they have even more force behind their hits. The Center for the Study of Retired Athletes studied the force of impact when college players hit each other. They recorded g-force impacts of almost 23 units—roughly four times the g-force a person would get while riding a roller coaster. Stronger hits can reach 100 units.[7]

Each season, between 4 percent and 20 percent of college football players get a concussion. More than one third of college players have had at least one concussion, and many have had more.[8] The average player also gets as many as 1,000 subconcussive hits to the head each season.[9]

For most of its history, the NCAA provided no rules to guide football teams when their players got a head

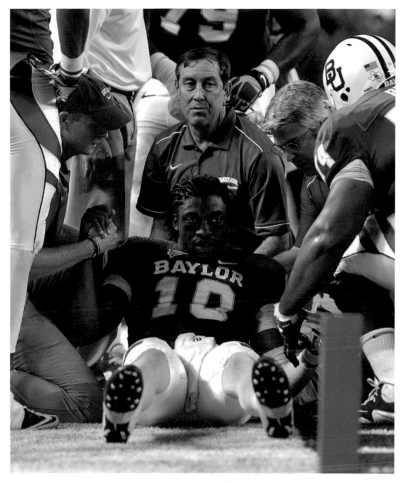

Baylor University quarterback Robert Griffin III is knocked out of a game. College players are at particularly high risk for concussions.

injury. But in the 2000s, researchers were starting to make discoveries that would challenge the idea that football players of any age are indestructible. They would turn everything the football industry thought it knew about concussions on its head.

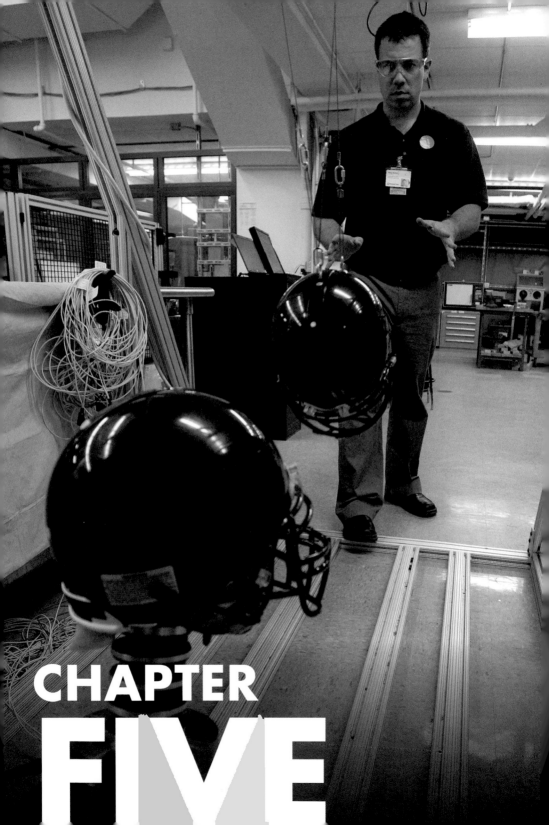

CHAPTER
FIVE

STUDYING BRAIN INJURIES

For many years, players and coaches knew very little about concussions and other brain injuries, although they were happening quite often. Even doctors and scientists knew little. Research on brain injuries did not begin in earnest until the 1980s, and the real breakthroughs did not happen until the 2000s.

A Silent Epidemic

On November 24, 1982, a *Wall Street Journal* article described concussions in football as "a silent epidemic."[1] The story started to open the public's eyes to the problem of brain injuries in sports. A lot of players were getting concussions, yet little was being done to prevent these injuries.

During the early 1980s, neuropsychologist Jeff Barth and other doctors at the University of Virginia saw more than 1,000 patients with concussions in

Concussion research has evolved—this high-tech study measures helmet-to-helmet force.

just two years. Barth decided it was time to study concussions. During his research, he discovered head injuries were often more serious than they seemed. He found that even people who did not lose consciousness could have a concussion, despite common belief. Many concussion sufferers had serious thinking and memory problems afterward.

Barth studied football players, a group he knew was likely to get head injuries. He tested University of Virginia football players, asking them to recognize words and put numbers in order. After a player sustained a head injury, Barth gave him the test again. Of the 2,350 players he examined, more than 8 percent suffered at least one concussion during the study.[2] The players with concussions had more trouble completing the same test after their injuries. Many of the players who sustained concussions had headaches, nausea, dizziness, and memory loss after their injuries. Even players without visible symptoms such as dizziness had difficulty thinking, remembering, and performing other brain functions.

Doctors were starting to learn a hit to the head was much more serious than just "getting your bell rung."

With the ImPACT Test, Mark Lovell, shown here, and Joe Maroon gave teams a quick tool to help diagnose brain injuries.

Research was revealing football hits could cause serious brain damage.

Testing the ImPACT

Although scientists were learning more about concussions, these injuries were still hard to detect. In the middle of a football game, coaches had a hard time telling whether a player had a concussion and needed to stay out of the game.

In the early 1990s, neurosurgeon Joe Maroon and neuropsychologist Mark Lovell at the University of Pittsburgh created a way to quickly identify a concussion. They came up with the ImPACT Test, a computerized test to measure a player's symptoms, memory, and reaction time after a hit to the head. ImPACT is so easy to administer, a team's trainer or doctor can give it to players right on the sidelines. They can use the test to decide whether to pull a player from a game.

The NFL's Committee

As evidence began linking football and concussions, the NFL, under commissioner Paul Tagliabue, hired its own researchers to investigate brain injuries and respond to the emerging research from independent groups. In 1994, it formed the Mild Traumatic Brain Injury (MTBI) Committee. For more than a decade, the committee would cause controversy.

In charge of the committee was Elliot Pellman, a rheumatologist. Many experts were perplexed about the NFL choosing Pellman to lead the committee. A rheumatologist treats people with muscle and joint injuries—not brain injuries.

Neurologists were aware Pellman lacked previous experience with brain science. One doctor said,

With the severe nature of brain injuries, many researchers questioned why a rheumatologist was leading the NFL's MTBI Committee.

I would hear [Pellman] say things in speeches like, 'I don't know much about concussions, I learn from my players,' and, 'We as a field don't know much about concussions,' and it used to bother me. We knew what to do about concussions, but he was acting like it was new ground.[3]

The Experts Gather

In 1996, sports medicine experts gathered in Pittsburgh to share what they had learned about concussions. The panel of doctors included Bailes, Maroon and Lovell, and Robert Cantu from the Boston University School of

Medicine. Joining them was a lineup of retired players. These included Pittsburgh Steelers and Chicago Bears running back Merril Hoge, New York Giants linebacker Harry Carson, Steelers quarterback Mike Tomczak, and Buffalo Bills safety Mark Kelso.

The doctors talked about the science behind brain injuries. The players talked about the reality of living with brain injuries. The players said they had spent their careers ignoring brain injuries. They did not ask to sit out after they were injured because they feared they would lose their jobs if they admitted they were

MERRIL HOGE

In 1994, while playing for the Chicago Bears, Hoge was running the ball toward the goal line when linebacker Derrick Thomas collided into him. "I've never been in an earthquake, but the first thing I thought was, 'Holy cow, man, the earth is shaking.'"[4] To check for a possible concussion, the trainer asked whether Hoge knew where he was. Hoge said he was in Tampa Bay because he thought he could hear the ocean. He was in Kansas City.

Soon after, Hoge suffered another hit to the head during a game against the Buffalo Bills. In the locker room, Hoge passed out and stopped breathing. The repeat injuries left Hoge with severe memory problems. He could not remember his two-year-old daughter's name. He would sometimes get lost walking from his house to his mailbox.

Hoge went to see Maroon and Lovell. They had tested his memory at the beginning of the season. Now, they checked it again. His scores had dropped by half. Maroon told Hoge his football career was over. Hoge retired from the NFL at the end of the 1994 season. He was only 29 years old.

hurt. "Players are interchangeable parts," Carson said. "Someone played your position before you, and when you leave, someone else is going to be in your place."[5]

In 1997, the American Academy of Neurology, an organization of brain specialists, examined all the concussion research. It confirmed repeated concussions can lead to brain damage. The academy released new guidelines for dealing with head injuries in sports. It recommended players who lose consciousness or have symptoms of a concussion—including a vacant stare, confusion, or slurred speech—be removed from the game. Players with mild concussions were advised to stay out of the game for one week. Those with severe concussions were to avoid playing for at least two weeks.

Studying Retired Athletes

Bailes wanted to learn more about the effects football had on the bodies and brains of former players. In 2000, he started the Center for the Study of Retired Athletes, a research center at the University of North Carolina. Kevin Guskiewicz, a former NFL trainer, helped him run the center.

To find out how brain injuries affect professional football players, Guskiewicz mailed surveys to more

Former players such as Joe DeLamielleure reported an alarming number of brain-injury complications affecting their everyday lives.

than 3,600 former players. Roughly 2,500 responded.[6] The survey included hundreds of questions about the concussions players had suffered during their careers.

The results were alarming. More than 60 percent of players responded they had sustained at least one concussion during their careers. Almost 25 percent said they had suffered three or more concussions. Players with repeat concussions were three times as likely to have serious memory problems as those who never had concussions.[7] Many of the players also reported they were depressed, had constant headaches, and did not hear or speak as well as they once did.

Bailes said this gave his team the first hint that football players had more than just brain injuries—they had a brain disease. And that disease would soon be discovered in a Pittsburgh morgue.

Chronic Traumatic Encephalopathy

When Omalu examined Webster's body on September 28, 2002, he made a major breakthrough in brain injury research. Webster was 50 years old when he died, yet Omalu discovered Webster's brain was filled with brown splotches—abnormal collections of a protein called tau. It is the same protein that builds up in the brains of much older people with Alzheimer's disease. No one had ever made such a discovery before. Omalu named this strange new disease chronic traumatic encephalopathy (CTE) and began studying it.

TAU PROTEIN

Tau protein is found in the nerve axons of every brain. Its job is to move messages down the axon to the next neuron. But when tau becomes damaged and spills out of the axons, it can lead to Alzheimer's disease. And when a head injury tears axons and releases tau into the brain, it can lead to CTE.

After a concussion, the brain does its best to clean up all the spilled tau proteins. But when the head is hit over and over again, the tau builds up, damaging the brain and leading to CTE symptoms such as memory loss and confusion.

Researchers now knew what CTE was, but they still did not know the exact injuries that led to this condition. How many times did a player have to get hit, and how hard did those hits have to be, to cause brain damage? Why did some retired players have memory loss and anger issues while others were perfectly fine?

These were just some of the questions scientists still needed to answer. And they needed to find out quickly, before more players suffered.

"I've called it a ticking time bomb," NFL agent Leigh Steinberg said of the growing number of brain injuries among football players. "If it's not addressed adequately, we might be consigning a whole generation of players to consciousness problems 30 years from now."[8]

But even with the research breakthroughs, the NFL did not respond to the problem as promptly and adequately as many had hoped.

CHAPTER
SIX

DENIAL AND RESISTANCE

Researchers were learning more and more about the long-term effects of brain injuries in football. And more and more news articles were covering football players with these injuries. It was becoming clear the football industry was in the middle of a serious concussion problem. The trouble was, the NFL was not ready to admit it had a problem.

The NFL protested when the media and researchers started calling for rule changes to protect players. "I think our fans want to see our players continue to play football the way they understand football should be played," said Art Rooney II, president of the Pittsburgh Steelers.[1] For years, that sentiment would keep the league from making real changes. And it would continue putting players at risk.

Patriots linebacker Ted Johnson received clearance to play too soon after a concussion—and suffered another one four days later.

"Medically Clear"

Despite the new research findings in the 2000s about concussions, players typically received the "medically clear" signal to return to the field too soon after suffering head injuries. But this practice was dangerous, as psychiatrist Arthur Lazarus stated:

> Every physician knows that the term 'medically' clear is meaningless. It only signifies that the person's heart is beating and the lungs are expiring—for now. It does not speak to the long-term (or even the short-term) prognosis of the injured player, and it gives a false sense of security that players are not in imminent danger.[2]

In 2002, New England Patriots linebacker Ted Johnson sustained a concussion during a preseason game against the New York Giants. Four days later, his coach, Bill Belichick, put him back on the field for full-contact practice. Even though Johnson did not feel well, he was afraid to say no to the coach. During the practice, Johnson was hit again and got another concussion. By 2007, he was suffering from depression, memory loss, and drug addiction.

Johnson's experience was not unique. It was happening all across the NFL, even with research indicating concussions were not to be treated lightly.

Often when a player sustained a head injury, team doctors and trainers did little more than a quick check to determine if he were fit enough, in their opinion, to play again. The only official rule in both professional and college football was that players who had been knocked unconscious could not return to the same game. However, players often had concussions even if they were not knocked out.

Injured players typically did little to protest when they were sent back into the game after an injury. In the NFL's culture of toughness, players knew full well the repercussions of asking to sit out. Sometimes the players seemed to have no choice but to follow orders. Nate Jackson, a former member of the Denver Broncos, stated, "Players have little control over their bodies; they are the property of the team."[3] According to *Philadelphia Inquirer* columnist Paul Davies, many times players did not protest because they were too afraid of losing their high-paying jobs:

> I understand why a pro football player would run back on the field minutes after suffering a concussion. The answer is money. And I understand why NFL team owners and coaches let players return to the game, and even encourage them to suck it up. The answer is more money.[4]

The NFL's Response

The NFL was concerned about the latest research about head injuries in football. Word was getting out in the media about CTE, this strange brain disease afflicting football players. "This is the league's worst nightmare," said retired Tampa Bay Buccaneer Dave Pear.[5] With billions of dollars a year at stake, the NFL had good reason to worry. News stories about football players losing their memory and killing themselves were not good for its reputation. There was also a concern about whether the NFL could be held liable in a lawsuit from injured players.

As asserted in *League of Denial* by Mark Fainaru-Wada and Steve Fainaru, the league attempted to twist the facts and findings. It had a response for nearly every other study. For instance, the league insisted the rate of concussions in the NFL had not risen since the 1980s, contrary to other evidence. "In the big picture, when you consider the number of times the head is impacted [in pro football], the number of concussions is relatively small," declared NFL director of communication Greg Aiello.[6]

The NFL also contradicted reports about players' injuries and even deaths. The league contended Webster did not die from CTE, but from a combination of alcohol, steroids, and drug abuse. They also argued Long, who had killed himself by drinking antifreeze, did not die due to injuries he had sustained on the field. Instead, it claimed he had suffered from years of substance abuse.

> "It's one thing to go out and play football and understand that when you turn 40, you can bend over to pick up your child and have aches and pains. It's another thing to bend down and not be able to identify that child."[7]
> —NFL agent Leigh Steinberg

MTBI Findings

At the forefront of the NFL's response was the MTBI Committee. First formed in 1994, the committee now had more than ten years of research. It published a series of studies on brain injuries in football players.

Under the MTBI Committee, players often returned to the game when
still suffering concussion symptoms, such as headaches and dizziness.

On one hand, the committee had promised to take steps to make football safer. It investigated new helmet designs that could reduce concussions. The committee also wrote up a new definition of concussion for team doctors and trainers. It described a concussion as "any traumatically induced alteration of brain function," which involved symptoms like dizziness, headaches, memory loss, and changes in personality.[8]

But on the other hand, the committee's findings were very different from other researchers' findings. Among many controversial assertions, the MTBI research suggested professional football players did not regularly take hits to the head and were not at much risk for concussions. It stated players could safely return to a game the same day of their injuries, even if they were knocked unconscious. It also claimed there was no evidence that multiple concussions led to more injury or cumulative effects. The committee pointed out that when players sustained concussions, they were back on the field in less than a week. According to the committee, that alone proved concussions were very mild—not that coaches and team doctors had rushed players back to the game too soon.

Many scientists researching brain injuries thought the committee's research was not just wrong, but dangerous. "I believe the findings of the NFL, as published, are definitely putting players at risk," said New York University neuropsychologist Bill Barr.[9] The NFL was on one side of the brain injury debate, and the research community was on the other. The two sides were about to go up against each other—head to head.

Concussion Summit

In 2006, Tagliabue retired after 17 years as NFL commissioner. Roger Goodell replaced him as the new commissioner. Under the new leadership, the NFL held its first-ever concussion summit in 2007. Doctors, trainers, and neurologists gathered in Chicago to debate the long-term effects of brain injuries on players. Goodell made the opening remarks. He pledged the NFL's commitment to reducing brain injuries in professional football.

Then the debate began. On one side were neurologists such as Bailes, Cantu, and Guskiewicz and neuropsychologist Barr. They were known to openly disagree with the NFL's research. Barr attacked the NFL's MTBI research. He claimed the league ignored important data that showed football players were at risk for concussions and CTE. To show what evidence the MTBI research seemed to be overlooking, Bailes presented slides of football players' brains filled with dark splotches of tau protein. He described the horrible symptoms plaguing former players: memory loss, depression, suicides.

Then neurologist Ira Casson, cochair of the MTBI Committee, had his turn. He challenged the assertion

HELP FOR PLAYERS

After years of providing little support to former players with dementia, the NFL established the 88 Plan in 2007. It was named in honor of Number 88, John Mackey, a former Indianapolis Colt. The fund provides $88,000 per year to former players with dementia who live in nursing homes and up to $50,000 a year for those who live at home. The plan has reimbursed approximately $7 million in medical expenses.

However, many players with dementia are not capable of applying for or are even aware of the 88 Plan. To this end, Gay Culverhouse, former Tampa Bay Buccaneers president, set up Players' Outreach Program to help players apply for the benefits.

NFL spokesman Aiello praised the Players' Outreach Program:

Part of our challenge has been finding the retired players who need help. Gay Culverhouse's efforts to help them is admirable, and we very much want to make the 88 Plan available to . . . retired players who should be getting it.[10]

At the concussion summit, new commissioner Roger
Goodell gathered experts and opened the debate.

that buildup of tau protein could have been caused by a
number of factors, including steroids or substance abuse.

"He was really digging in and just totally unwilling
to budge, and that was really their view on everything,"

said Barr of Casson's response. "[It was] like, 'Okay, I'll listen to you, but you're wrong. We gave you a chance to talk today, but you're wrong.'" The concussion summit did not produce any immediate resolutions. But according to Guskiewicz, the debate was "the game changer, the turning point."[11] Even if the two sides were still in conflict, the issue was now out in the open.

NO PROOF

Casson concluded there was no proof playing football caused brain damage. In fact, he seemingly argued successful former football players were "proof" the game did not cause brain damage:

> The public has been led to believe that dementia and depression are a frequent and inevitable consequence of a career in professional football. This 'false fact' is belied by the presence of a large number of retired players who, despite experiencing multiple concussions, have gone on to have brilliant careers in broadcasting and other endeavors.[12]

CHAPTER
SEVEN

A SENSE OF VICTORY

Brain injury researchers were finding the NFL more resistant than they expected. But on their side was a formidable ally: Chris Nowinski, a former Harvard football player and professional wrestler. "Chris Harvard," as he was known on the World Wrestling Entertainment circuit, was on a crusade to make football a safer game. He knew firsthand the damage players were suffering.

A Center for CTE Research

Nowinski knew that to make real changes in football, researchers would need even more evidence about the dangers to players. They needed to know the risks of concussions and how widespread CTE was in former players.

In 2008, Nowinski joined forces with neurologist Cantu. Together, they met with Bob Stern, a professor

Thanks to Chris Nowinski, families began donating the brains of recently deceased players to CTE research.

CHRIS HARVARD

After playing defensive tackle for the Harvard football team, Nowinski became a professional wrestler, fighting in the ring under the name Chris Harvard. By the time he was in his late 20s, Nowinski had been tackled, smacked, and punched in the head countless times. He had terrible headaches, blurred vision, and depression.

After seeing a series of doctors, Nowinski realized his years of football and wrestling had left scars deep inside his brain, where no one could see them. In 2006, he wrote *Head Games: Football's Concussion Crisis* to alert the public to the problem of head injuries in football.

of neurology at Boston University. The three set up an entire department at Boston University just to study the brains of former football players. It was called the Center for the Study of Traumatic Encephalopathy. To head the research, they chose Ann McKee, a neurologist and pathologist. McKee was a big football fan, and she was more than ready to embark on this new field of study.

However, McKee could not find CTE in the brains of live football players. CTE did not show up on any X rays or other brain scans. It was impossible to detect CTE without cutting open the brain. McKee needed brains from recently deceased players. But where could she get them? The answer came from Nowinski. Upon hearing of players' deaths, Nowinski asked the families if the players had experienced depression,

With efforts from (*from left*) Stern, McKee, Nowinski, and Cantu, the Center for the Study of Traumatic Encephalopathy found CTE evidence in players' brains.

memory loss, and other signs of CTE before they died. He encouraged them to donate the players' brains to science.

"This Is Going to Change Football"

Nowinski's calls worked. As donations came in, McKee had many brains to study. She examined tiny slivers of brain tissue under a microscope. In February 2008, she examined the brain of John Grimsley, a former linebacker for the Houston Oilers. His brain was full of

tau protein. She also found tau in the brain of former
Tampa Bay Buccaneers lineman Tom McHale, who
had died of a drug overdose. By 2012, McKee would
examine the brains of 34 former NFL players. In 33 of
the 34 brains, she found brown clumps of tau protein
similar to those Omalu had first found in Webster's
brain.[1]

DAVE DUERSON

After retiring in 1993,
Chicago Bears defender
Dave Duerson was on
track for a successful new
career. But soon his business
closed, his house went into
foreclosure, and his wife
divorced him after a battery
charge. On February 17,
2011, police found Duerson
dead from a gunshot wound.
In a suicide note, he wrote,
"My mind slips. Thoughts
get crossed. Cannot find my
words . . . I think something
is seriously damaged in my
brain."[4] Duerson shot himself
in the chest, sparing his
brain because he wanted
it donated to science.
He knew something was
terribly wrong.

McKee knew how important
these discoveries were. "It's a
crisis, and anyone who doesn't
recognize the severity of the
problem is in tremendous
denial," she said.[2] At one point,
she remarked, "This is going to
change football."[3]

The damage McKee saw in
the players' brains was unique
to people who had sustained
repeated head injuries. Even
players who had not had
concussions showed evidence
of CTE. That meant smaller
subconcussive hits to the head
could also cause permanent

brain damage over time. "I have never seen this disease in any person who doesn't have the kind of repetitive head trauma that football players would have," McKee said.[5] When asked how many professional football players she thought had CTE, she guessed the percentage would be shocking.

But middle-aged, former professional football players were not the only ones affected. McKee also found evidence of CTE in the brains of young college players—and even in high school players—who had died. She saw it in the brain of Eric Pelly, a high school football player who died at age 18 after suffering two concussions. "The findings are very shocking because we never thought anybody that young could already be started down the path to this disease," said Cantu. "It should send a powerful message to people at every level of football that they need to care about this issue and treat concussions with respect."[6]

All the Way to Congress

The evidence was mounting, and the link between football and brain injuries was getting stronger. The debate would go all the way to Congress. On October 28, 2009, the House Judiciary Committee, a congressional committee that enforces criminal laws and constitutional amendments, held hearings on brain damage in football. The NFL as a business is a type of monopoly that can come under federal scrutiny, such as the House hearings.

The committee was concerned with the NFL's treatment of its former and current players, but also with the effect the league's policies had on younger players. Committee chair John Conyers, a Democrat from Michigan, stated:

> I say this not simply because of the impact of these injuries on the 2,000 current players and more than 10,000 retirees associated with the N.F.L. and their families. . . . I say it because of the effect on the millions of players at the college, high school and youth levels.[7]

Goodell was there to defend the league's policies. He said the NFL was doing everything it could about the problem. "I can think of no issue to which I've devoted more time and attention than the health and well-being of our players, and particularly retired players," he told the committee.[8] On the other side of the debate, Nowinski, McKee, Cantu, and Bailes testified about the dangers of head injuries in sports. Former NFL players such as Hoge, Tiki Barber, and George Martin spoke as well.

Some members of Congress accused the NFL of hiding the dangers of football. "The NFL sort of has this blanket denial or minimizing of the fact that there may be this link," said Linda T. Sánchez, a Democrat from California. "And it sort of reminds me of the tobacco companies pre-'90s when they kept saying, 'Oh, there's no link between smoking and damage to your health.'"[9]

Other committee members once again stressed this denial at the NFL level also put the younger players at risk. Congressman Hank Johnson of Georgia said,

THE TOBACCO INDUSTRY

As the NFL denied claims and research about brain injuries, many people compared its actions to the tobacco industry's. In the 1950s, nearly half of Americans smoked. But then independent research started highlighting the dangers of smoking. In response, the tobacco industry created its own research group, the Council for Tobacco Research. The council put out study after study trying to deny the link between smoking and lung cancer.

In the 1990s, documents were leaked showing the tobacco industry had known for many years its products were dangerous and addictive. Nearly every state sued the tobacco industry. In November 1998, tobacco companies agreed to pay billions of dollars to cover health-care costs for illnesses caused by smoking.

Congress members considered the trickle-down effect of the NFL's concussion policy on high school and youth players.

Walking off the pain in an N.F.L. game turns into walking it off in a Little League game—the trickle-down effects on high school and college players are very real and can be fatal.[10]

Dick Benson spoke on behalf of parents with children playing high school football. His teenage son died of bleeding in his brain in 2002 after suffering several concussions while playing high school football. Benson tearfully begged the committee to take action so such a death would not happen again.

The congressional hearings were a major turning point in the crusade to make football safer. In a matter of weeks, changes would start happening in the NFL—and beyond. After years of the NFL denying the research and real-life experiences of former players suffering with brain injuries, "it was the turning point," said Nowinski. "I mean, the only way to say it is, you changed their mind. In a sense, it was a victory."[11]

FAMILIES SPEAK OUT

Also at the hearings were family members of former NFL players. Eleanor Perfetto's husband, Ralph Wenzel, was a former offensive tackle for the Pittsburgh Steelers and San Diego Chargers. He was diagnosed with Alzheimer's disease in 1999. "He can no longer dress, bathe or feed himself," Perfetto told the committee. "Frankly my husband no longer has a life. And he does not have a life that he and I want for anyone else."[12] After his death in 2012, Perfetto donated Wenzel's brain to the Center for the Study of Traumatic Encephalopathy, where McKee confirmed evidence of CTE as well as Alzheimer's.

CHAPTER
EIGHT

A SHIFT IN FOOTBALL

Just a few weeks after the congressional hearing, the NFL radically shifted its position on brain injuries. In a *New York Times* article, an NFL spokesperson admitted the league now understood the seriousness of concussions. In December 2009, Goodell announced the NFL would instate new rules and procedures in an effort to better protect players from brain injuries. It marked the beginning of a shift after many years of "no pain, no gain" and "tough it out" attitudes.

New Rules, New Awareness

Under the old rule, teams held players out of games only if the players had been knocked unconscious. But the new rule stated players were not to return to the game if they had any signs of a concussion. If a player was found to have a concussion, the new rule declared he could not return to the game until both his team doctor and an

The new rules were the first positive steps for the NFL to protect players from the dire consequences of concussions.

independent neurologist, who didn't work for the team, cleared him.

To make the new guidelines clearer, the NFL hung a poster in each team's locker room warning players about the dangers of concussions. It listed common concussion symptoms, such as balance problems, headache, and dizziness. And it urged players to report any of these symptoms to their trainer or team doctor right away.

A few months later, on March 16, 2010, the NFL replaced the controversial MTBI Committee with the NFL Head, Neck and Spine Medical Committee, a new group to study concussions. To head the committee, they chose two respected brain surgeons: H. Hunt Batjer of Northwestern Memorial Hospital at Northwestern University and Richard Ellenbogen of Harborview Medical Center at the University of Washington.

IMMEDIATE RESULTS

The new rules in December 2009 seemed to create some positive effects almost immediately. The week before the changes, Pittsburgh Steeler Ben Roethlisberger and Arizona Cardinal Kurt Warner sustained head injuries and were expected to play in their upcoming games. But under the new guidelines, their teams ultimately held the players out. "The evidence demonstrates that team medical staffs have been addressing concussions in an increasingly cautious and conservative way," Goodell stated.[1]

The committee's job is to use the latest research to help prevent and treat concussions in NFL players.

These changes were just the beginning. Over the next few years, the NFL would institute several new rules—everything from raising awareness about brain injuries to monitoring and treating players for injuries.

FINING HARD HITS

Fans, coaches, and players have cheered for big hits and crushing tackles for years. But in the new era of concussion awareness, the NFL took steps to stop glorifying these hard hits that lead to brain injuries. To this end, the league created new rules about hits to the head.

In October 2010, three players were fined for dangerous hits: Pittsburgh Steelers linebacker James Harrison, New England Patriots safety Brandon Meriweather, and Atlanta Falcons cornerback Dunta Robinson. Some players had mixed feelings about the new rules. Meriweather said of his fine,

They teach you growing up that you've got to be violent and put the fear of God in people, but when you get to the league that you've been dreaming about your whole life, they tell you to change your game 100 percent or get money taken from you.

Other players and officials felt the tougher rules were long overdue. "Time has changed, and our emphasis has changed," said Ray Anderson, the NFL's executive vice president of football operations.[2]

Monitoring and Treating Players

The NFL changed the way football players are monitored for brain injuries—even before the season begins. At the start of every season, team doctors must now examine each player and test his memory, concentration, attention, reaction time, and balance to establish a baseline score. If a player suffers a head injury during the season, the doctors can consult the baseline score to determine whether the player is healing or showing signs of more serious damage. "The most important thing is knowing what [a player] was like before a concussion," said physician Stan Herring of the Seattle Seahawks.[3]

Players are also carefully monitored during games. Athletic trainers watch for any hit that might cause a concussion. That player is then removed from the game, and the team's medical staff thoroughly checks him.

Gone are the days of holding up a couple fingers for a player to count. Whenever a player suffers a possible head injury, the team doctor must look for a checklist of symptoms, including loss of consciousness, confusion, trouble balancing, and memory loss. The doctor will also ask the player a series of questions, such as where the team is playing and the team's previous opponent.

Under the new guidelines, injured players receive extensive testing to determine if they have sustained a concussion.

If a player has a possible concussion, he must leave the field and go to the locker room.

Players with concussions get medical treatment and are required to rest until their symptoms are gone. Then a team doctor will give the player more tests to determine progress. "Some guys may come back in a week. Some guys may come back in six weeks," said Herring. "The player's history of injury and other issues come into play."[4]

Changes to the Game

As part of its commitment to making football safer, the NFL also introduced several new rules governing game play. One rule prohibits a player from hitting an opponent with the crown, or the very top, of the helmet. This prevents players from turning their helmets into weapons that can injure. Anyone caught violating the rule gets a penalty for unnecessary roughness. Players also cannot make contact with opponents after a play has been called dead.

In addition, the NFL instituted new rules for kickoffs. In the past, the kicking team would run for 40 yards (36 m) or more during kickoffs. That long run gave them time to build up a lot of force with which to tackle the kickoff returner. The NFL moved kickoffs from the 30-yard

NO TOLERANCE FOR CONCUSSIONS

Even football fans are beginning to change their attitudes about concussions. In 2010, Indianapolis Colts receiver Austin Collie was knocked unconscious with two concussions six weeks apart. Five days after his second concussion, many reporters and fans were calling for him to retire. "Why is concussion-prone Austin Collie still in NFL?" asked one headline. The article suggested Collie "could be dying right before our eyes."[5]

Despite the risks he faced, Collie had no intention of retiring at age 25.

With kickoffs often resulting in forceful, violent hits, even a rule change of five yards can reduce concussion risk.

(27 m) line up to the 35-yard (32 m) line and limited the kicking team to a five-yard (4.6 m) running start, so the tacklers cannot build up as much force. Experts believe the small changes will lead to a big reduction in player injuries. "When the league makes any small change, like changing the kickoff by five yards, those five yards will remarkably reduce the amount of concussions," said McKee.[6]

Protecting Young Players

The NFL's shift toward protecting players from brain injuries had long-reaching effects. The new NFL rules also inspired new rules to protect high school and college football players.

A 2009 study from Nationwide Children's Hospital in Ohio found that as many as 40 percent of high school athletes were returning to the game too soon after a concussion.[7] One year later, the National Federation of State High School Associations released new guidelines. Now any student who shows signs of a concussion—such as headaches, dizziness, confusion, or balance problems—needs to be removed from the game immediately. That student cannot play football again until a doctor confirms he is concussion-free. Almost every state has adopted new concussion laws that uphold these guidelines.

Similar to the NFL, college football teams and many high school teams also now test their players at the beginning of each season. Then they retest them a few times during the season to detect possible brain injuries and monitor progress.

Positive Steps Forward

Players of all ages were seeing changes that hoped to make the game of football safer. As Goodell stated,

> This . . . reinforces our commitment to advancing player safety. Along with improved equipment, better education, and rules changes designed to reduce impacts to the head, it will make our game safer for the men who play it, and set an important example for players at all levels of play.[8]

Continued research and rising awareness could bring even more changes regarding football and brain injuries. In fact, the future of football as fans know it is being questioned.

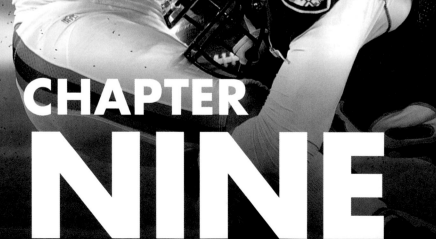

CHAPTER
NINE

THE FUTURE OF FOOTBALL

The new rules and procedures are steps in the right direction, but football still remains a risky sport. The potential for life-changing brain injuries is still high. Researchers continue searching for answers, and advocates continue challenging the NFL to protect its players. But the question still remains: With brain injuries being a serious concern, what is the future of football?

Continuing Research

By 2013, McKee had examined the brains of nearly 50 deceased NFL players. Most of them showed evidence of CTE. Even though her work had made great strides, she said there was still much to learn about brain injuries in football. "It's going to require the analysis of many hundreds of brains," she said. "That's so important. We've learned so much from every brain donation."[1]

In order to truly protect players from brain injuries, does the entire game of football need to change?

Also in 2013, researchers at UCLA made a major breakthrough. They identified tau protein in the brains of living players. They used a new kind of brain imaging scan to examine the brains of former Vikings linebacker Fred McNeill, former Chargers quarterback Wayne Clark, and three other players. All five players had tau concentrated in areas of the brain that control memory and emotions. "I've been saying that identifying CTE in a living person is the Holy Grail for this disease and for us to be able [to] make advances in treatment," said

NEW HELMET DESIGNS

A major factor in brain safety is, of course, the helmet. With continuing research, many new helmet designs have emerged over the years in an attempt to prevent injuries. The Xenith has shock absorbers. The Gladiator has a carbon-fiber frame and a foam covering. And the Bulwark has five panels that can be configured to fit each player's needs.

In 2000, the NFL hired Biokinetics, an engineering company, and Riddell, a sports equipment manufacturer, to produce the ultimate helmet to dramatically reduce the risk of a concussion. The Revolution became the most widely used helmet in the NFL. College, high school, and youth leagues also used it.

Yet from the beginning, Biokinetics warned the NFL that no helmet could completely protect the brain. "The best helmets in the world don't stop rotational forces, where the brain whips around and snaps back," Cantu explained.[2] That is why even the best helmets today come with a warning sticker that reads: "No helmet system can protect you from serious brain and/or neck injuries including paralysis or death. To avoid these risks, do not engage in the sport of football."[3]

Bailes, who worked on the study. "The findings are preliminary—we only had five players," added Gary W. Small, the study's lead author, "but if they hold up in future studies, this may be an opportunity to identify CTE before players have symptoms so we can develop preventative treatment."[4]

Another potential breakthrough occurred in early 2014. Researchers from the University of Rochester identified how levels of S100B, a brain protein, rise after a concussion. S100B levels can be tested with a simple blood test taken with a finger prick. More research is needed after these preliminary results, but the findings could mean teams may someday be able to diagnose concussions with a quick test moments after a hit.

The NFL Has to Pay

The congressional hearings of December 2009 first shed light on the NFL's alleged denial about brain injuries. As evidence of CTE in football players grew, 4,500 individuals—retired players and the families of deceased players—filed a lawsuit against the NFL in 2013.[5] They claimed the league knew repeated collisions led to permanent injuries but did little to prevent the problem.

Participating in the lawsuit was the family of retired San Diego Chargers linebacker Junior Seau, who killed himself in 2012. Once one of the league's premier players, Seau's brain tested positive for CTE. As his family said in a statement:

> While Junior always expected to have aches and pains from his playing days, none of us ever fathomed that he would suffer a debilitating brain disease that would cause him to leave us too soon.[6]

In August 2013, the NFL settled the case for $765 million.[7] The money helped cover exams for retired players, health-care costs for players who suffered brain injuries, and concussion research and education. NFL attorney Jeff Pash said in a statement, "This is an important step that builds on the significant changes we've made in recent years to make the game safer."[8] One thing the NFL did not do, however, was officially admit any guilt. In fact, the NFL stated the settlement "does not represent, and cannot be considered, an admission by the NFL of liability, or an admission that plaintiffs' injuries were caused by football."[9] And while opponents have long accused the NFL of hiding evidence about brain injuries, the settlement did not require the league to release any internal documents.

The Future of Youth Football

With increased awareness about brain injuries, the public now realizes football safety needs to start with its very youngest players. Some experts think children should play modified games such as flag football and avoid tackle football entirely. Cantu argues children should not play tackle football until age 14.

To help youth and their coaches learn how to prevent concussions, USA Football—the governing body for youth, high school, and amateur football—started the Heads Up Football program. This organization helps train youth football coaches and players in safer tackling techniques and concussion awareness. As of 2013, nearly 2,800 youth

NFL FUNDS CONCUSSION RESEARCH

In support of brain injury research, the NFL earmarked more than $100 million for Harvard Medical School. The money will go toward a 10-year study of more than 1,000 retired players.[10] And the NFL will give General Electric and Under Armour $60 million for a four-year study called the Head Health Initiative.[11] The research will look into new imaging techniques to detect brain injuries and better-designed equipment to help prevent them.

The NFL also pledged a much smaller donation of $1 million to the Center for the Study of Traumatic Encephalopathy.[12] It promised to encourage players to donate their brains to the center upon their deaths.

Former NFL quarterback Jake Plummer speaks with young players on behalf of Heads Up Football.

football leagues representing approximately 600,000 players across the country had signed up for Heads Up Football.[13]

The future of youth football will greatly impact the future of the NFL and football as a whole. It takes a high volume of children in youth and high school football programs to produce the high-level players needed in the NFL. "If only 10 percent of [parents] in America begin to conceive of football as a dangerous game, that is the end of football," said Maroon.[14]

There is already evidence that parents are afraid to let their children play tackle football. Participation in Pop Warner football, the biggest youth football program in the United States, dropped 9.5 percent between 2010 and 2012.[15] Fear about head injuries was the number one reason parents did not enroll their children in the program. Even President Barack Obama weighed in: "I'm a big football fan, but I have to tell you if I had a son, I'd have to think long and hard before I let him play football."[16]

Could Football Come to an End?

Experts are still looking at ways to make football safer. But many realize that truly protecting football players from injury means changing the whole nature of the sport. And that realization worries a lot of people.

Some people are beginning to wonder: Could the epidemic of brain injuries eventually bring an end to the game? Would fans even like football if the necessary safety changes were made? "Thirty years from now, I don't think [professional football] will be in existence," said Baltimore Ravens safety Bernard Pollard. "There's going to come a point where fans are going to get fed up with it."[17]

Might Americans one day look back on football as a barbaric relic, much like the gladiator fights in ancient Rome? Could football eventually be considered so dangerous it is banned entirely? Given the current popularity of the sport and the money it generates, that seems unlikely.

But nevertheless, people are taking a closer look at the sport and thinking carefully about the best—and safest—ways to play it. In an October 2013 letter to fans, Goodell stated,

> We are proud that the game is safer and more exciting today than ever, but we are never satisfied. In keeping with our history, we are committed to pursuing a path that ensures the rewards of playing football continue to far outweigh the risks.[18]

The future of the NFL may be decided by parents choosing—or not choosing—to let their children play football.

But as a researcher seeing the tragic effects of football firsthand, McKee has another perspective. "Football is an American sport. Everyone loves it. I certainly would never want to ban football," she said. "We haven't banned cigarette smoking. People smoke. People make that choice. But they need to make an informed choice."[19]

TIMELINE

1905
Nineteen football players die, including
17-year-old Vernon Wise in November.

1943
The NFL makes wearing helmets mandatory.

1982
On November 24, the *Wall Street Journal* describes
concussions in football as a "silent epidemic."

1994
The NFL creates the Mild Traumatic
Brain Injury (MTBI) Committee.

1994
The "Season of the Concussion" sees many
injuries, including three quarterbacks
knocked unconscious on October 25.

1997

The American Academy of Neurology releases new guidelines for treating brain injuries in sports.

2000

Julian Bailes starts the Center for the Study of Retired Athletes.

2002

Former Pittsburgh Steeler Mike Webster dies of a heart attack on September 24.

2002

On September 28, Bennet Omalu finds evidence of chronic traumatic encephalopathy in Webster's brain.

2004

On September 30, former Steeler Justin Strzelczyk kills himself during a high-speed police chase.

2006

Former Philadelphia Eagle Andrew Waters commits suicide on November 20.

TIMELINE

2006
Paul Tagliabue retires as NFL commissioner, and Roger Goodell replaces him.

2007
The NFL holds its first ever concussion summit in June.

2008
Boston University establishes the Center for the Study of Traumatic Encephalopathy.

2008
Chris Nowinski begins encouraging families to donate the brains of deceased players to science.

2009
On October 28, the House Judiciary Committee holds hearings on brain damage in football.

2009
The NFL issues new stricter rules on concussions in December.

2010

The NFL Head, Neck and Spine Medical Committee replaces the MTBI Committee on March 16.

2010

Teenager Nathan Stiles suffers a concussion on October 1 that would lead to his death.

2012

On May 2, former NFL linebacker Junior Seau commits suicide.

2013

Researchers at UCLA find tau protein in the brains of living NFL players.

2013

In August, the NFL settles a lawsuit by former players and their families for $765 million.

2014

Researchers from the University of Rochester identify a rise in the S100B brain protein during concussions.

ESSENTIAL FACTS

At Issue
- Independent research has found that hits to the head in football lead to concussions, which can cause permanent injuries.

- Young football players' brains are even more vulnerable to damage than adults' brains.

- In 2002, researchers identified chronic traumatic encephalopathy (CTE), a disease found in the brains of former professional football players.

- Beginning in 2009, the NFL changed its stance on brain injuries, instituting new rules to protect and treat players.

Critical Dates
1900s to 1980s
In the earliest days, players had next to nothing to protect them from brain injuries. Helmets evolved over the years, but players still put their brains at risk. After years of concussions, players suffered from memory loss, depression, and personality changes. Even researchers did not fully understand brain injuries.

1982 to 2002
The *Wall Street Journal* called concussions the "silent epidemic" in football. Researchers began studying brain injuries. Their findings suggested players were causing serious long-term damage to their brains. In response, the

NFL launched its own research committee, which published controversial conclusions.

2002 to 2009
In a major breakthrough, Bennet Omalu discovered Mike Webster suffered from CTE. Researchers focused on learning about this new disease. When Roger Goodell became NFL commissioner in 2007, he opened the debate about concussions. But overall, the NFL resisted making significant changes.

2009 to present
With heightened awareness of concussions, the US House Judiciary Committee held hearings on brain damage in football. This resulted in immediate changes in the NFL, college football, and beyond, and more changes continued. In 2013, the NFL settled a major lawsuit with former players and their families. The future of football may be in question: Will players ever be safe from brain injuries?

Quote
"I've called it a ticking time bomb. If it's not addressed adequately, we might be consigning a whole generation of players to consciousness problems 30 years from now."
—*NFL agent Leigh Steinberg*

GLOSSARY

delusional
Having false beliefs.

dementia
A severe form of memory loss caused by disease or injury to the brain.

dissenter
A person who does not agree with an established opinion.

incoherent
Being unclear and hard to understand.

monopoly
Exclusive possession of a service or product market.

neurologist
A doctor who studies the brain and how it works.

neuropsychologist
A doctor who studies brain function to determine why people act the way they do.

neurosurgeon
A doctor who performs surgery on the brain.

paranoid
Being unreasonably suspicious or untrusting of others.

ADDITIONAL RESOURCES

Selected Bibliography

Associated Press. "Goodell Issues Memo Changing Return-to-Play Rules for Concussions." *NFL.com*. NFL, 2 Dec. 2009. Web.

Bartholet, Jeffrey. "The Collision Syndrome." *Scientific American* 306.2 (Feb. 2012): 66–71. Print.

Fainaru-Wada, Mark, and Steve Fainaru. *League of Denial: The NFL, Concussions and the Battle for Truth*. New York: Crown, 2013. Print.

Garber, Greg. "NFL Players in Harm's Way." *ESPN*. ESPN, 27 Jan. 2004. Web.

Further Readings

Editors of *Sports Illustrated*. *Sports Illustrated Football's Greatest*. New York: Sports Illustrated, 2012. Print.

Guess Mckerley, Jennifer. *Football: Science Behind Sports*. Farmington Hills, MI: Lucent, 2012. Print.

Hudson, Maryann. *Concussions in Sports*. North Mankato, MN: ABDO, 2014. Print.

Websites

To learn more about Essential Issues, visit **booklinks.abdopublishing.com.** These links are routinely monitored and updated to provide the most current information available.

Places to Visit

Center for the Study of Retired Athletes

Department of Exercise and Sport Science
University of North Carolina
209 Fetzer Hall, CB#8700
Chapel Hill, NC 27599-8700
888-830-4885
http://exss.unc.edu/research-laboratories/center-for-the-study-of-retired-athletes
Formed by neurologist Julian Bailes, the center studies the lasting effects former football players experience.

Center for the Study of Traumatic Encephalopathy

Boston University School of Medicine
Robinson Complex
Suite 7800
Boston, MA 02118
http://www.bu.edu/cste
Located at Boston University, the center is a leading research facility examining the brains of deceased players.

SOURCE NOTES

Chapter 1. Iron Mike

1. Greg Garber. "Man on the Moon." *ESPN*. ESPN, 26 Jan. 2005. Web. 30 Mar. 2014.

2. "Mike Webster: Reader's Digest." *Dignity After Football*. Dignity After Football, 6 Apr. 2011. Web. 30 Mar. 2014.

3. Mark Fainaru-Wada and Steve Fainaru. *League of Denial: The NFL, Concussions and the Battle for Truth*. New York: Crown, 2013. Kindle Fire.

4. Ibid.

5. Peter King. "One Team, 25 Years On." *Sports Illustrated*. Time, 12 Dec 2011. Web. 30 Mar. 2014.

Chapter 2. Inside Brain Injuries

1. Jeffrey Kluger. "Headbanger Nation." *Time*. Time, 31 Jan 2011. Web. 30 Mar. 2014.

2. David Pittman. "Need More Study on Concussions, IOM Says." *MedPageToday*. MedPageToday, 31 Oct 2013. Web. 30 Mar. 2014.

3. Harrison S. Martland. "Punch Drunk." *JAMA* 91.15 (13 Oct. 1928): 1103. Print.

4. Tom Foster. "The Helmet Wars." *Popular Science*. Popular Science, 18 Dec 2012. Web. 30 Mar. 2014.

5. Greg Garber. "Concussions Still Carson's Concern." *ESPN*. ESPN, 7 Feb. 2010. Web. 30 Mar. 2014.

6. Ben McGrath. "Does Football Have a Future?" *New Yorker*. Condé Nast, 31 Jan. 2011. Web. 30 Mar. 2014.

7. Jeffrey Kluger. "Headbanger Nation." *Time*. Time, 31 Jan. 2011. Web. 30 Mar. 2014.

8. Carroll Cole. "Uncovering Concussions: How They're Changing Our Brains and the Game." *Chicago Health Online*. Northwest Publishing, n.d. Web. 30 Mar. 2014.

Chapter 3. Football Takes Its Toll

1. Peter King. "Concussions." *Sports Illustrated*. Time, 1 Nov. 2010. Web. 30 Mar. 2014.

2. Mark Fainaru-Wada and Steve Fainaru. *League of Denial: The NFL, Concussions and the Battle for Truth*. New York: Crown, 2013. Kindle Fire.

3. Ken Reed. "It's Time to Ban High School Football." *Chicago Tribune*. Tribune Newspapers, 29 Aug. 2012. Web. 30 Mar. 2014.

4. John Underwood. "An Unfolding Tragedy." *Sports Illustrated*. Time, 14 Aug. 1978. Web. 30 Mar. 2014.

5. Whet Moser. "A Brief History of Football Head Injuries and a Look Towards the Future." *Chicago Magazine*. Chicago Tribune, 4 May 2012. Web. 30 Mar. 2014.

6. Christopher Klein. "How Teddy Roosevelt Saved Football." *History*. A&E Television Networks, 6 Sept. 2012. Web. 30 Mar. 2014.

7. "Nov 12, 1892." *History*. A&E Television Networks, n.d. Web. 30 Mar. 2014.

8. Travis Waldron. "The NCAA's History with Concussions: A Timeline." *ThinkProgress*. ThinkProgress, 23 July 2013. Web. 30 Mar. 2014.

9. Ibid

10. Brian Dalek. "The Evolution of the Football Lineman." *Men's Health*. Rodale, 4 Jan. 2013. Web. 30 Mar. 2014.

11. Mark Fainaru-Wada and Steve Fainaru. *League of Denial: The NFL, Concussions and the Battle for Truth*. New York: Crown, 2013. Kindle Fire.

12. Timothy Gay. *Football Physics: The Science of the Game*. Emmaus, PA: Rodale, 2004. Print. 32.

13. Greg Garber. "NFL Players in Harm's Way." *ESPN*. ESPN, 27 Jan. 2004. Web. 30 Mar. 2014.

14. Ibid.

15. Mark Fainaru-Wada and Steve Fainaru. *League of Denial: The NFL, Concussions and the Battle for Truth*. New York: Crown, 2013. Kindle Fire.

Chapter 4. Dangers to Young Players

1. Rick Maese. "Tackling a Crisis." *Washington Post*. Washington Post, 24 Oct. 2013. Web. 30 Mar. 2014.

2. Patrick Dorsey. "Helmet Tech Aimed at Concussions." *ESPN*. ESPN, 1 Sept. 2009. Web. 30 Mar. 2014.

3. Carroll Cole. "Uncovering Concussions: How They're Changing Our Brains and the Game." *Chicago Health Online*. Northwest Publishing, n.d. Web. 30 Mar. 2014.

4. Jeffrey Kluger. "Headbanger Nation." *Time*. Time, 31 Jan. 2011. Web. 30 Mar. 2014.

5. "Sports-Related Head Injury." *American Association of Neurological Surgeons*. American Association of Neurological Surgeons, Dec. 2011. Web. 30 Mar. 2014.

6. "Concussions." *American Academy of Pediatrics*. American Academy of Pediatrics, n.d. Web. 30 Mar. 2014.

7. Jeffrey Kluger. "Headbanger Nation." *Time*. Time, 31 Jan. 2011. Web. 30 Mar. 2014.

8. "Concussion." *American Association of Neurological Surgeons*. American Association of Neurological Surgeons, Dec 2011. Web. 30 Mar. 2014.

9. Jeffrey Kluger. "Headbanger Nation." *Time*. Time, 31 Jan. 2011. Web. 30 Mar. 2014.

Chapter 5. Studying Brain Injuries

1. Mark Fainaru-Wada and Steve Fainaru. *League of Denial: The NFL, Concussions and the Battle for Truth*. New York: Crown, 2013. Kindle Fire.

2. Ibid.

3. Michael Farber. "The Worst Case." *Sports Illustrated*. Time, 19 Dec. 1994. Web. 30 Mar. 2014.

4. Matt Crossman. "Lost." *Sporting News* 231.26 (25 June 2007). Print.

5. Patrick Hruby. "The Wrong Man for the Job." *Sports on Earth*. MLB Advanced Media and USA TODAY, 16 May 2013. Web. 30 Mar. 2014.

6. Mark Fainaru-Wada and Steve Fainaru. *League of Denial: The NFL, Concussions and the Battle for Truth*. New York: Crown, 2013. Kindle Fire.

7. Kevin M. Guskiewicz, et al. "Association Between Recurrent Concussion and Late-Life Cognitive Impairment in Retired Professional Football Players." *Neurosurgery* 57.4 (2005): 719. Print.

8. Mark Fainaru-Wada and Steve Fainaru. *League of Denial: The NFL, Concussions and the Battle for Truth*. New York: Crown, 2013. Kindle Fire.

9. Ibid.

10. "Amyotrophic Lateral Sclerosis." *PubMedHealth*. A.D.A.M., 26 Aug. 2012. Web. 30 Mar. 2014.

Chapter 6. Denial and Resistance

1. Ben McGrath. "Does Football Have a Future?" *New Yorker*. Condé Nast, 31 Jan. 2011. Web. 30 Mar. 2014.

2. Arthur Lazarus. "NFL Concussions and Common Sense: A Recipe for Medical Errors and a Lesson for Physician Leaders." *Physician Executive* 37 (Jan.–Feb. 2011): 6. Print.

3. Nate Jackson. "The NFL's Concussion Culture." *Nation*. Nation, Aug. 15–22, 2011. Web. 30 Mar. 2014.

SOURCE NOTES CONTINUED

4. Paul Davies. "Ringside: Is Playing Football Worth the Risk of Injury?" *Philly*. Philadelphia Media Network, 19 Sept. 2010. Web. 30 Mar. 2014.

5. Ben McGrath. "Does Football Have a Future?" *New Yorker*. Condé Nast, 31 Jan. 2011. Web. 30 Mar. 2014.

6. Mark Fainaru-Wada and Steve Fainaru. *League of Denial: The NFL, Concussions and the Battle for Truth*. New York: Crown, 2013. Kindle Fire.

7. Eddie Pells. "Agent: Concussions Are 'Ticking Time Bomb.'" *Lubbock Avalanche-Journal*. Lubbock Avalanche-Journal, 21 Apr. 2007. Web. 30 Mar. 2014.

8. Mark Fainaru-Wada and Steve Fainaru. *League of Denial: The NFL, Concussions and the Battle for Truth*. New York: Crown, 2013. Kindle Fire.

9. Peter Keating. "Doctor Yes." *ESPN*. ESPN, n.d. Web. 30 Mar. 2014.

10. "88 Plan Overview." *NFL Player Care Foundation*. NFL Player Care Foundation, n.d. Web. 30 Mar. 2014.

11. Mark Fainaru-Wada and Steve Fainaru. *League of Denial: The NFL, Concussions and the Battle for Truth*. New York: Crown, 2013. Kindle Fire.

12. Ibid.

Chapter 7. A Sense of Victory

1. Lauren Ezell. "Timeline: The NFL's Concussion Crisis." *PBS*. WGBH, 8 Oct. 2013. Web. 30 Mar. 2014.

2. Bob Hohler. "Major Breakthrough in Concussion Crisis." *Boston Globe*. Boston Globe, 27 Jan. 2009. Web. 30 Mar. 2014.

3. Mark Fainaru-Wada and Steve Fainaru. *League of Denial: The NFL, Concussions and the Battle for Truth*. New York: Crown, 2013. Kindle Fire.

4. Ibid.

5. Peter King. "Concussions." *Sports Illustrated*. Time, 1 Nov. 2010. Web. 30 Mar. 2014.

6. Bob Hohler. "Major Breakthrough in Concussion Crisis." *Boston Globe*. Boston Globe, 27 Jan. 2009. Web. 30 Mar. 2014.

7. Alan Schwarz. "N.F.L. Scolded over Injuries to Its Players." *New York Times*. New York Times, 28 Oct. 2009. Web. 30 Mar. 2014.

8. Ibid.

9. Ibid.

10. Alan Schwarz. "N.F.L.'s Influence on Safety at Youth Level is Cited." *New York Times*. New York Times, 29 Oct. 2009. Web. 30 Mar. 2014.

11. Mark Fainaru-Wada and Steve Fainaru. *League of Denial: The NFL, Concussions and the Battle for Truth*. New York: Crown, 2013. Kindle Fire.

12. Associated Press. "Goodell Defends NFL on Concussions." *CBS News*. CBS, 28 Oct. 2009. Web. 30 Mar. 2014.

Chapter 8. A Shift in Football

1. Associated Press. "Goodell Issues Memo Changing Return-to-Play Rules for Concussions." *NFL.com*. NFL, 2 Dec. 2009. Web. 30 Mar. 2014.

2. Damon Hack. "Learning to Play Nice." *Sports Illustrated*. Time, 24 Oct. 2011. Web. 30 Mar. 2014.

3. "NFL's 2013 Protocol for Players with Concussions." *NFLEvolution.com*. NFL, 1 Oct. 2013. Web. 30 Mar. 2014.

4. Ibid.

5. Greg Doyel. "Why Is Concussion-Prone Austin Collie Still in NFL? He's Like His Dad." *CBS Sports*. CBS, 23 Aug. 2012. Web. 30 Mar. 2014.

6. Damon Hack. "Learning to Play Nice." *Sports Illustrated*. Time, 24 Oct. 2011. Web. 30 Mar. 2014.

7. Preston Williams. "High School Football Coaches Get an Education on Concussions at Redskins Park." *Washington Post*. Washington Post, 30 Apr. 2010. Web. 30 Mar. 2014.

8. Associated Press. "Goodell Issues Memo Changing Return-to-Play Rules for Concussions." *NFL.com*. NFL, 2 Dec. 2009. Web. 30 Mar. 2014.

Chapter 9. The Future of Football

1. Andy Thompson. "Appleton Native in Center of Concussion Debate." *Fox11*. FOX 11 WLUK, 2 Dec. 2013. Web. 30 Mar. 2014.

2. Paul Solotaroff. "This is Your Brain on Football." *Rolling Stone*. Rolling Stone, 31 Jan. 2013. Web. 30 Mar. 2014.

3. Ken Belson. "Warning Labels on Helmets Combat Injury and Liability." *New York Times*. New York Times, 4 Aug. 2013. Web. 30 Mar. 2014.

4. Steve Fainaru and Mark Fainaru-Wada. "CTE Found in Living Ex-NFL Players." *ESPN*. ESPN, 22 Jan. 2013. Web. 30 Mar. 2014.

5. Sheena Harrison. "Despite Football Concussion Settlement, Insurers Role in Paying NFL Costs Unclear." *Business Insurance*. Crain, 9 Sept. 2013. Web. 30 Mar. 2014.

6. Jason M. Breslow "Family of Junior Seau Files Wrongful Death Suit Against NFL." *PBS*. WGBH, 23 Jan. 2013. Web. 30 Mar. 2014.

7. Associated Press. "NFL, Ex-players Agree to $765M Settlement in Concussions Suit." *NFL. com*. NFL, 29 Aug. 2013. Web. 30 Mar. 2014.

8. Sheena Harrison. "Despite Football Concussion Settlement, Insurers Role in Paying NFL Costs Unclear." *Business Insurance*. Crain, 9 Sept. 2013. Web. 30 Mar. 2014.

9. Ibid

10. Stephanie Smith. "NFL Players Association, Harvard Planning $100 Million Player Study." *CNN*. Time, 29 Jan. 2013. Web. 30 Mar. 2014.

11. NFL. "GE-NFL Head Health Challenge Continues." *NFL.com*. NFL, 1 Aug. 2013. Web. 30 Mar. 2014.

12. Associated Press. "NFL Partnering with BU Study." *ESPN*. ESPN, 20 Dec. 2009. Web. 30 Mar. 2014.

13. Gary Mihoces. "High Schools Adopting Heads Up Football Program." *USA Today*. USA Today, 11 Aug. 2013. Web. 30 Mar. 2014.

14. Mark Fainaru-Wada and Steve Fainaru. *League of Denial. The NFL, Concussions and the Battle for Truth*. New York: Crown, 2013. Kindle Fire.

15. John Gever. "Striking a Nerve: Shift Seen in Kids' Football." *MedPageToday*. MedPageToday, 30 Nov. 2013. Web. 30 Mar. 2014.

16. Franklin Foer and Chris Hughes. "Barack Obama Is Not Pleased." *New Republic*. New Republic, 27 Jan 2013. Web. 30 Mar. 2014.

17. "Bernard Pollard: NFL's Future Bleak." *ESPN*. ESPN, 28 Jan. 2013. Web. 30 Mar. 2014.

18. Roger Goodell. "Roger Goodell Explains Commitment to Make NFL Safer." *NFL Evolution*. NFL, 4 Oct. 2013. Web. 30 Mar. 2014.

19. Mark Fainaru-Wada and Steve Fainaru. *League of Denial: The NFL, Concussions and the Battle for Truth*. New York: Crown, 2013. Kindle Fire.

INDEX

ABOUT THE AUTHOR

Stephanie Watson is a freelance writer based in Providence, Rhode Island. Over her 20-plus-year career, she has written for television, radio, the web, and print. Stephanie has authored dozens of young adult nonfiction books, including *Pope Francis: First Pope from the Americas; Mystery Meat: Hot Dogs, Sausages, and Lunch Meats—The Incredibly Disgusting Story;* and *Understanding Obesity: The Genetics of Obesity.*

ABOUT THE CONSULTANT

Dr. Elad I. Levy, MD, FACS, FAHA, FAANS, is a board-certified neurosurgeon who joined the Department of Neurosurgery at the University of Buffalo in 2004 and is now a full professor of Neurological Surgery and Radiology. He completed his neurosurgical training at the University of Pittsburgh and received his medical degree from George Washington University School of Medicine. Dr. Levy is the creator of the Program for Understanding Childhood Concussion and Stroke (PUCCS). His objective is to bring awareness to coaches, parents, and the entire Western New York community about the devastating effects a major concussion can cause in children.